GW00419678

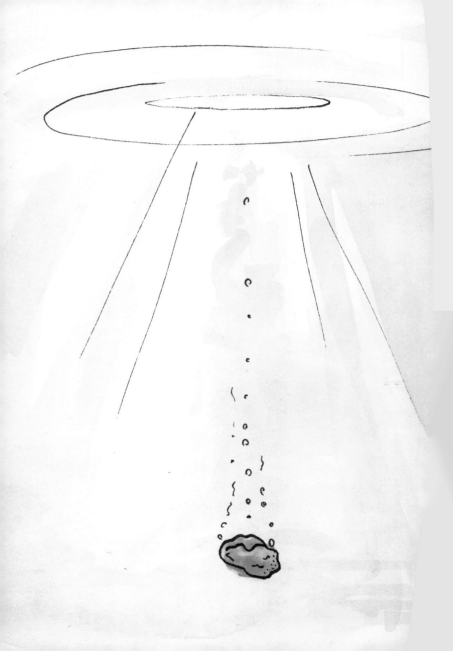

Written by

JASON GRAHAM

Go Within or Go Without

Stepping Stones on the Journey Home

*Visual expressions
and book design by*

GIULIA PIGNONE

www.gowithingowithout.com

Contents

Acknowledgements

Infinite love and gratitude to my fiery-haired angel,
Lynsey for your unceasing love, care and guidance –
without you I would still be looking.

To my creative partner, Giulia for your energy,
patience and, most of all, your brilliance in bringing
the poems to life.

To my Beloved Master, Mooji for opening me up
to self-enquiry. Om Namah Shivaya.

Jason Graham

Foreword

Jason's poetry is a potent reminder that we need look no further than here. Whatever it is we're seeking – awakening, enlightenment, peace of mind – can't be found by searching. *What if, / for all your hard work, / you were missing a trick?* Exactly. It is, as Jason points out, a matter of remembering, rather than attaining or gaining. And life invites us to remember in each moment, at every turn.

I first met Jason at one of Tim Freke's Mystery Experience weekends, several years ago. During that weekend, we experienced first-hand the paradox that lies at the heart of life. Jason's poems capture this paradox beautifully, in a way that only poetry can. We're one, and yet we're many. *That One, / faceless / yet in every smile / heartless / yet in every beat / homeless yet home to all...* his lines express the ineffable knowing that comes when we find ourselves in the deep mystery.

Neither does Jason neglect the pain of separation and illusion, the deep longing that we come face to face with at some point on our journeys. Poems like *Life, Lust* and *Self Sentence* articulate the dilemma of the separate self within a few lines. We all know what it's like to feel chained by our desires, or dictated to by our thoughts. These words clearly arise right out of Jason's immediate experience, and nothing is excluded. It's all here, from the mundane to the sublime.

9

Giulia's visual expressions add a sweetness and humour to the poems that make this book a delight to hold, as well as to read. Her touching illustrations underline the poignancy and real humanity of poems such as *Laid Bare* and *A New Beginning*.

This book is truly an invitation to go within, to discover the richness that's already here. When we dare to do so, we find that we no longer have to go without, for we're no longer lacking; *...where you are / is where you've always wanted to be, / and who you are is / all you've ever dreamt of being.* We finally come home to the mystery for ourselves, over and over. Thank you, Jason.

Fiona Robertson,
Senior Facilitator/Trainer of the Living Inquiries
August 2014

www.beyondourbeliefs.org
www.whilstwalkingjack.blogspot.com

An Introduction

Where are you in your life, now?

Looking, searching, seeking
you appear to be everywhere
but here;
wanting, trying, striving
you long to be anyone
but you.

What if,
for all your hard work,
you were missing a trick?
What if there's an easier way,
One that is
infinitely more rewarding?

Life never stops inviting you
to at least look this way,
if only to find where you are
is where you've always wanted to be,
and who you are is
all you've ever dreamt of being.

What if,
by chance,
this was one such invitation?
Rather than dismiss, discard, delay,
what better time to accept
than NOW?

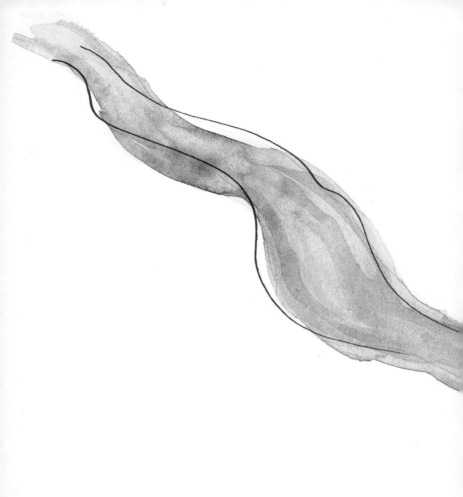

Sleeping

With my brain washed
in society's hands
the truth slips
beyond my grasp.

The Hunter

Full with hunger
I caged my heart
and let my mind loose
hunting the things of this world
in vicious circles.

Flesh, paper, concrete, cloth
I devoured them all
yet every taste of success
only left me wanting more,
taking me further and further afield.

Newsflash

Tired from sleeping
I appear happy
picking up stories from a news-agent;

happy resting my head in another's hands,
their words forming the thoughts
that dislocate my actions.

Child's Play

Growing up
I saw life as a toy
a transformer
that appeared only to change
endlessly
yet never stopped being
more than my heart desired.

Now I am a man
I have forgotten
I am
born to play
endlessly –
if only I could get out of my head
and return.

Overflowing with creative energy

yet begging for inspiration,

am I never to realise

the true art of life hiding within

the formlessness of just being?

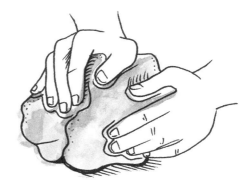

Blank Page

Sleepless
without her soothing touch,
I wonder
will tonight be the night
she returns to caress me
until I am ready to create?

Frustrated
by her continued absence,
I fake her presence
playing with words
sensing
she's watching…

waiting
silently
between the lines
of worn out words
fit only to clutter
the trash can of my mind;

out of sight
but trapped in thought,
she remains untouchable
in the one place
she can be touched
at will.

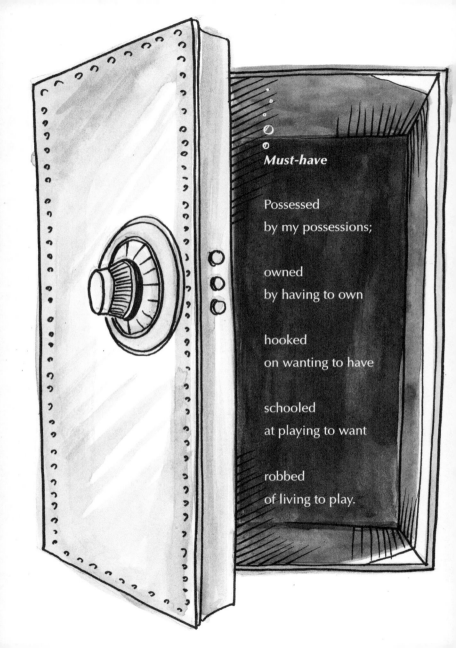

Must-have

Possessed
by my possessions;

owned
by having to own

hooked
on wanting to have

schooled
at playing to want

robbed
of living to play.

Life

Locked in

the chain of desire

I clatter around

like a convict

separated

from what I long for most

resigned to chasing illusions.

．
。
。
O
o
Lust

Distracted by your absence,

You who satisfies me completely,

I am reduced

to craving your touch

over and over again.

A Match Made in Heaven

In my manic search for an ideal mate
I have neglected to realise
I am cheating myself
from the perfect love that dwells within.

But with a mind that's been coaxed
to believe its better half is out there,
I'd end up all alone
if I remembered that.

Always thinking

yet do you ever think

to stop…

to think about the unthinkable

beyond your thoughts?

The Dictator

Beneath the engulfing shadow of security
I have created a rogue state
where my thoughts dictate
I will never be safe.

But with a mind that's preoccupied
taking care of me,
I'd be care-less
if I remembered that.

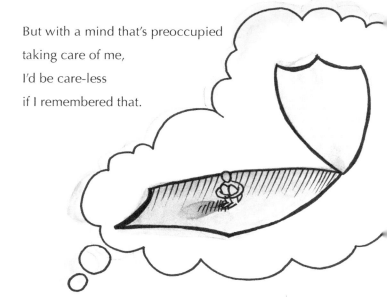

Cold Comfort

In the comfort
of your security
lies the insecurity
of your desires
so why do you desire
to be secure?

Priceless

Consumed by an idea
about the nature of It,

that It can be
taken or bought
given or sold,

freedom will always come
at the cost of freedom.

A Day Out

While we spend our day at the beach
splashing around on the surface
the mystery lying beneath
is forever
imploring us to dive deeper.

Restless

"Who are you?"
I was asked
and I answered...

You are simply unreal
I am no stranger
yet still you must ask:

Who am I?

Staring into space
do you not see
or at least glimpse my face?

In your emptiness
do you not feel
or at least sense my presence?

If only you would
you would no longer
seek, beg nor long;

If only you would
you would finally rest
and never sleep again.

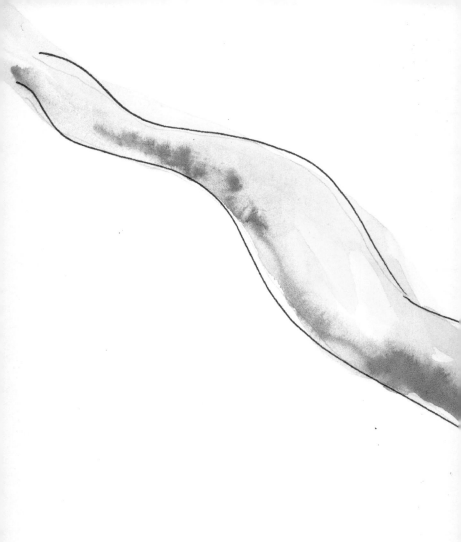

Stirring

I long to witness
one loving
One-Self
without a surgeon in sight.

Laid Bare

Let's just strip
you and me,
let's just lie down here
and strip
layer after layer

until overcome
by the scentless
intoxicating fragrance
of what is,
we lose ourselves

in the moment.

Senseless

If all I could see
was in front of my eyes

I'd be blind.

If all I could hear
was the sound that noise makes

I'd be deaf.

If all I could feel
was the touch of another

I'd be numb.

And if the only way to my heart
was through my stomach

I'd be sick.

But it's not
because I AM.

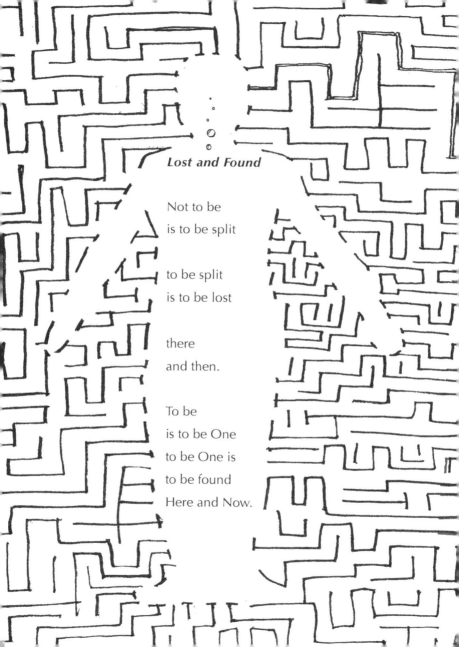

Lost and Found

Not to be
is to be split

to be split
is to be lost

there
and then.

To be
is to be One
to be One is
to be found
Here and Now.

Expecting Love
to arrive in the form
of another
is like the ocean
awaiting a wave
to give it water.

The More the Merrier

Under the ravenous spell of desire
I have become gluttonous
wanting more of this
craving more of that.

But with a mind kept hungry
by the promise of fulfillment,
it would leave me empty
to remember that.

Self Sentence

Prisoner to approval
I sit in the corner of my cell
painting pretty pictures of myself

overflowing with creative energy
yet begging for inspiration,
am I never to realise
the true art of life hiding within
the formlessness of just being?

Will I ever dare
go beyond the rusting bars
where freedom sits, waiting...

like a mother unable to cradle her young?

I Am That

Who are you
That One,

faceless
yet in every smile

heartless
yet in every beat

homeless
yet home to all –

who are you
That One?

Runaway

In my endless pursuit of knowledge
I have become tireless,
determined to leave wisdom
lagging way behind.

But with a competitive mind
judged on its ability to know,
I would look stupid
if I remembered that.

— The End —

Head Hunting

You are not
still there
trapped in a place
you choose to work
ungodly hours,

haunted by not being
up to scratch
driven
by a pat on the back –
are you?

You do know
your home is here
in this space
where you are
perfect, as you are

free from all thoughts
of promotion
empty
of all emptiness –
don't you?

What good are words

when what needs to be said

can never be spoken?

Missing in Action

Deserted

to explore a dry, barren landscape

where the big brand roams ruthlessly

bellowing calls to action

promising

to make this world a better place;

a place where the me in me thrives

and I and I can't help but remain

indifferent

watching from my oasis.

Beneath the comforting blanket of approval
I find it easy to hide
the uncomfortable truth:
I don't really approve of myself.

But with a mind that's wired
to the network,
I'd be cut off
if I remembered that.

Like

Bird Feed

Why are you still sleepwalking
around the cage floor of your mind
when the door remains open?

Wake up;

dust your neglected feathers
and prepare to soar
without fear of falling
only to fall helplessly within
the untravelled
sky of your being.

Silent Witness

Unrecognised

or simply unknown

I can be found

witnessing the play

unnoticed

by a captivated cast –

unmoved

by their performance

I remain silent

and the stage lights slowly fade.

*The moment
you stop searching
is the moment
you find the One.*

A New Beginning

Let's make a stand
one last stand
against the fear
of failure
against the need
to succeed.

Let's make a stand
one last stand
for wanting
fighting
lacking less;
having
sharing
for Being
more…

…for trusting
not busting
dancing
not striving
creating
not surviving –
let's make the stand for evolving

not revolving
by surrendering
not remembering
receiving
not believing
shining
not whining.

Let's just make the stand
for letting go
of fearing
dying;
for standing aside
and embracing
loving
healing.

Then, standing as One
let's celebrate making that stand

for the falling
and the rising.

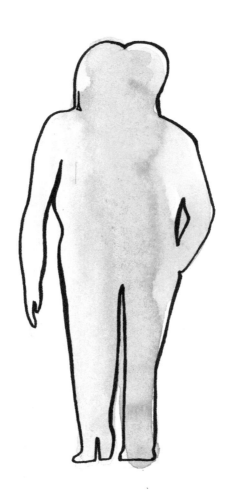

Without

you and me

there Is

nothing

between us.

Love Is in the Air

Love lies not hidden
in the rose bed of marriage
but within
and without
the rose and the bed.

Falling Apart

Just one look
a glance
pierced my resistance
left me wide open
resigned to my fate

Just one touch
a brush
shattered my world
left me in pieces
made me whole again.

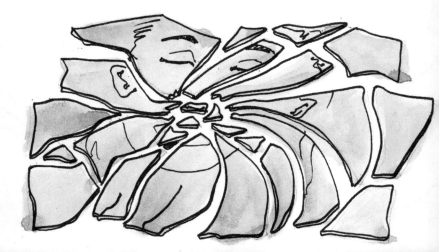

Enchanted

Saturated

with longing

fascinated

by nothing,

I am falling.

Breathless

in your presence

faceless

in your embrace,

I have fallen.

Thoughtless

Always thinking
yet do you ever think
to stop…
to think about the unthinkable
beyond your thoughts?

Now
imagine you stopped…
just for the moment
and in the thoughtless silence
you heard a secret

and imagine…
when you next thought
you did so aware:
you are the nothing
thinking to life your everything –

imagine that.

Great Expectations

Climbing
before I could walk
I was born to dream,
raised to expect
more or less.

I was led to believe
I can be
better than I am;
to be something
is to have something –

an object lesson
pushing me
to slowly carve myself
a career, making me rich
parents proud and society right.

Yet success didn't come
without teaching me a lesson:
while I was kept busy
climbing all over the floor
greatness was left hanging in the air.

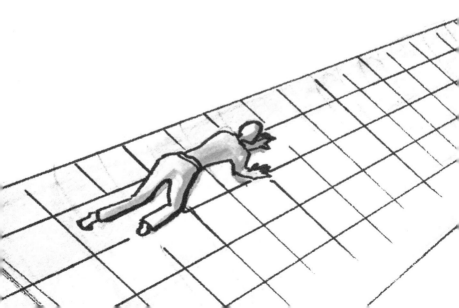

After lifetimes of chasing

all the things you want

you finally realise

you can never have

the One thing you want most.

Slow Dancing

What price a tear
torn from its hiding place
and lovingly asked to dance?

Without sound
it's a dance
in which you flow

without steps
it's a dance
in which you fall

deeper and deeper
within
without another to hold

moving as you move
from this world to that,
it's a lonely dance

as you step back
and tiptoe beyond
your swirling mind

overflowing with grace –
it's the one
in which you remember

you are not just the dancer
but the stage
on which the dance is taking place.

Blooming

Wrapped in the scent

of an isolated flower,

to-ing and fro-ing

here and there,

reflecting

I am alone

but never lonely.

Blooming

Wrapped in the scent
of an isolated flower,
to-ing and fro-ing
here and there,
reflecting
I am alone
but never lonely.

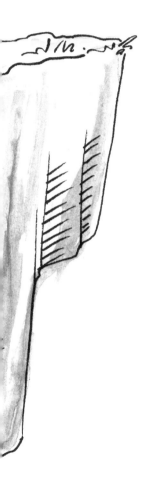

With my soles worn out
my pockets empty
I've arrived
at that place we fear
is always just a moment away.

Sick from striving to prevent
what will be
I've given up,
accepting I am
not to be with you.

My time is here
to surrender to what is
and realise it really isn't
the end of life
only the end of me.

Living Without Me

Without breathing
I breathe,

Without touching
I touch,

Without healing
I heal,

Without loving
I love –

Is there anything I can't do
without?

Broken

Today, something snapped
I felt it go

I remembered I am
and I am not.

Today, I became certain
of uncertainty

tomorrow lost its grip
and yesterday choked.

Today, Love broke through
and left fear paralysed

something finally snapped
I felt it go.

Speechless

What good are words
when what needs to be said
can never be spoken?

Dressed to take you out
stripped
to turn you in

they come in many guises
all intent on doing
whatever is asked

but, if you want the truth,
they will always remain
a waste of breath –

brush them off
let them be
who's there to care?

Just stay quiet
as you do
and listen to hear

That, which remains
disguised as wordless whispers
forever calling you home

Untouchable

Yesterday appeared to be
the beginning of the end,
growing meant touching life less
and less without conditions:

a child lost to schooling
unbounded potential crushed in Sir's clumsy grasp –
I soon learned that life is
nothing without conditions.

Tomorrow may be
full of promise but...
no real hope
without conditions:

a seeker seeking to find himself
in a world where he will remain lost –
I imagine life to be
nothing without conditions.

Today is
to touch without touching,
realising life is nothing yet everything
without conditions:

as I am, I will be –
unconditional being
my only condition
NOW.

The Two of Us

As we toy with the idea of love
let's do so carelessly
for She will never stop
offering a hand,

although, untouched

She will also never tire
of simply watching us play –
it's been much the same
since You and I was born.

Yet I feel, just like you
it will be much the same
until we grow tired
enough to care,

until we stop

turning away whenever She whispers
"sweet nothings",
masking rather than facing the idea
You and I are just a game.

I am

always

here.